CONFIDENCE AMID CHAOS

Mark Finley
with
Steven Mosley

Pacific Press Publishing Association
Boise, Idaho
Oshawa, Ontario, Canada

Edited by B. Russell Holt
Designed by Tim Larson
Cover photo by Steven Mosley
Typeset in 10/12 New Century Schoolbook

Copyright © 1992 by
Pacific Press Publishing Association
Printed in the United States of America
All Rights Reserved

Unless otherwise stated, all Scripture references
come from the New International Version.

Library of Congress Cataloging-in-Publication Data:

Finley, Mark, 1945-
     Confidence amid chaos / Mark Finley with Steven
Mosley.
          p.   cm.
     ISBN 0-8163-1131-5
     1. Bible—Prophecies. 2. Daniel (Biblical prophet) 3.
Christian life—1960-   4. Finley, Mark, 1945-   . I. Mos-
ley, Steven R., 1952- . II. Title.
     BS647.2.F45   1992
     220.1'5—dc20

                                        92-31631
                                           CIP

92 93 94 95 96 • 8 7 6 5 4

Contents

Introduction

The rapid pace of unfolding world events indicates our planet is on the verge of something unexpected—and tremendous. In recent months, we have witnessed some of the most astounding changes in human history. The freedom movements in Eastern Europe, the fall of the Berlin Wall, and the collapse of Communism caught us all by surprise. For the first time, a major world power has crumbled without a large-scale war. The dissolution of the former Soviet Union has left the United States as the world's only superpower.

What is the real truth behind the fall of Communism?

One fact is clear. A divine hand has certainly been guiding. God has been at work! Totalitarian regimes have been swept away. Authoritarian rulers have been overthrown. And doors for the proclamation of the gospel are wide open! During large evangelistic meetings in cities such as Belgrade, Budapest, and Moscow, I have seen thousands accept the gospel. Truly, this has been God's doing.

Nevertheless, there is another factor that must be seriously considered. Recent revelations in the news media indicate that the United States government conspired with Rome to hasten the demise of Communism. *Time* magazine called this one of the great secret alliances of all time. What is really going on? Where is our world headed? Are we moving toward a United States of Europe controlled by religious powers? Will the religious freedoms we have enjoyed in America ever be removed? Is there a mastermind of evil attempting to shape world affairs to his own ends? How can we possibly stand through earth's final crisis?

God's people will not be caught by surprise. The biblical prophecies clearly reveal the future. They unmask Satan's plans and reveal God's plans. They clearly describe the rise of the beast power, the enforcement of an economic boycott—a time when no one can buy or sell unless they receive the mark of the beast—the union of church and state to remove our historic freedoms, and Satan's final strategy.

But the prophecies also describe the outpouring of God's Holy Spirit in mighty power with thousands accepting Christ and His truth. They graphically portray a group of people so totally committed to Christ that they would rather die than be disloyal. The prophecies of Daniel and Revelation focus especially upon Christ's sustaining power—upon His faithfulness to His people during the time of their greatest trials.

In these pages, you will discover a new vision of the living Christ. You will be drawn to Him in a new way! Your faith in Him will increase. Your devotion to Him will deepen.

I wish to express special appreciation to my colleague, Steven Mosley, for his creative research and editorial insights, which are interwoven throughout this book. Together, Steve and I pray that God will use this little volume to prepare you spiritually for the crisis at the close. May the Christ of Revelation fill you with courage as you read these pages.

Mark A. Finley

Headed for Captivity

Jeremy Levin's world turned upside down when he was captured by Shiite Muslims and held hostage in Lebanon's Bekaa Valley. Jeremy, the Beirut bureau chief for CNN, felt isolated, helpless, and afraid. The only time he saw another human being was when his captors escorted him to the bathroom once a day. Crouched in the corner of a windowless room hour after hour, month after month, Jeremy desperately needed to talk. But he was afraid that if he talked with himself, he would go crazy. So he considered the idea of talking to God.

At first, this made him feel uncomfortable. Although he was the grandson of a rabbi, Jeremy had decided long before that he could believe only in concrete things—things he could touch and feel. He had rejected his Jewish religious heritage.

But with so little to touch and feel in that lonely cell, Jeremy eventually reached out to God—and began talking. Soon he realized that he was having a meaningful, two-way conversation. He tried hard to remember the bits of religious instruction he'd picked up in his youth. He remembered, too, what he had heard about the teachings of Jesus. Finally, everything began to fit together and make sense. He saw that Jesus Christ was truly the divine Son of God.

And that's when Jeremy faced a big choice. He had made the leap of faith; now how was he going to live? Jeremy decided, he later wrote, "You can't play games by assuming the external trappings while holding back from total acceptance." This tough newsman, a former atheist, said, "I decided it was necessary to accept it all. It had to be all or nothing."

And it was all for Jeremy Levin. His life was changed. Eventually he managed to escape his captors and was reunited with his family. But he had already experienced an even more significant reunion. Jeremy didn't merely survive the ordeal, he came out of it a new man—a new man in Jesus Christ.

You and I may never be held hostage by terrorists as was Jeremy Levin. But each of us faces difficult and discouraging situations of our own. How can we successfully endure the ordeals we face? To understand how we can survive, and even thrive, in the midst of trials, let's go back and take a look at another Hebrew hostage, a young man held captive in Babylon. The challenge this hostage faced was rather different from Levin's experience. It wasn't a meager diet or primitive living conditions that threatened to wear him down. It was the very opposite—a table loaded with the best that Babylon could offer.

Daniel's captors were trying to win him over to their side. This is how it began.

When the young Hebrew walked through the splendid gates of Babylon as one of a trail of captives following behind victorious King Nebuchadnezzar, he heard this kind of mockery: "If your God is the true god, why is Jerusalem in ruins? Why couldn't He protect you from us? Why did He allow you to go into captivity?"

These must have been extremely difficult questions to answer. After all, the Babylonians had sacked Jehovah's sacred temple and brought its precious vessels to this heathen city. It seemed as if the God of Abraham, Isaac, and Jacob couldn't defend even His own city—Jerusalem.

I believe these questions are relevant for us today. We're living in a world in which religious values and secular values increasingly clash. And, all too often, the secular values are winning. The spiritual seems more and more crowded out by other voices, other images. Sometimes our culture seems almost hostile to religion.

In some ways, those with religious principles seem like aliens in a strange land. It's my conviction that this tension will increase, not decrease, as time goes along. In fact, I believe this conflict will soon come to a tremendous climax as we near the end of earth's history. The astounding biblical prophecies of Daniel and Revelation predict that God's people will face captivity and imprisonment in earth's last hours.

So the question of how to survive as a hostage is very relevant to anyone interested in surviving the time of the end. Each of us will have to face that challenge: Where is your God? If He's so powerful, how come you're in so much trouble? Why can't He defend His people in the "real world"?

The book of Daniel contains some remarkable prophecies about how history will come to a climax. It gives us a picture of last-day events. But it does more. This book also shows us *how* to live in the time of the end. The stories of the book of Daniel reveal the character qualities of faith, courage, prayer, and perseverance necessary for living just before the coming of Christ.

In these chapters, we're going to blend the stories of Daniel with the prophecies of Revelation.

King Nebuchadnezzar had a special strategy to win the allegiance of the Hebrew hostages. It included a process of reeducation or brainwashing. We read about it in Daniel 1:3, 5: "The king ordered Ashpenaz, chief of his court officials, to bring in some of the Israelites from the royal family and the nobility.... They were to be trained for three years, and after that they were to enter the king's service."

Nebuchadnezzar wanted to turn the best of the Hebrew young men from hostages into Babylonian civil servants. They were to be educated in the customs, practices, and principles of Babylon. They were to study its science, its religion, its philosophy. And finally, when they'd been thoroughly indoctrinated, they would be sent back to their nation to rule for Babylon.

Nebuchadnezzar didn't always place Babylonians as rulers over conquered territories; that would only encourage rebellion. Instead he selected native people from these places to be trained in Babylon so they would rule their own captive cities—as his puppets.

Surprisingly enough, this is the situation in which many of God's people will find themselves as we near the close of time. Satan is bent on world conquest, of that we can be sure. His kingdom is in mortal combat with the kingdom of Christ. It's a war between the forces of good and the forces of evil. In an attempt to destroy our inner longings for God, Satan attempts to capture our thoughts through the senses.

He is working to submerge our world in a thoroughly secular culture. We see that everywhere, from the agnosticism of much of Europe to the growing materialism of Asia and the erosion of spiritual values in the United States. We are being indoctrinated in a secular world view, in a secular philosophy, in a secular way of life.

So how do we resist this pervasive influence? How do we stand for the kingdom of Christ in the midst of a culture that's often hostile to it? Lonely Daniel, the Hebrew hostage in a strange land, gives us the first important clue.

Once Daniel and his companions reached Babylon, the pressure to conform began to build. We can see that in the new names given to the Hebrew captives. When a Hebrew mother named her child, the name most often stood for character qualities she desired the child to have or for some significant aspect of Hebrew history. The name consistently reminded the child of his allegiance to the true God. Daniel's name, in Hebrew, means "God is my judge." This young man's name continually reminded him that he lived before the God who sees all things. But the head of the eunuchs in Babylon gave him the name Belteshazzar, meaning "Bel protect his [the king's] life." His friend, Hananiah ["the Lord is gracious"], was named Shadrach, meaning "inspiration of the sun." Mishael ["God-like"] was now called Meshach, "like [the god] Aku." And Azariah ["God is my helper"] received the name Abednego, meaning "servant of Nebo." Nebuchadnezzar wanted these Israelites to forget their Hebrew heritage, so he gave them names representing the false gods of Babylon.

We can see from this that Nebuchadnezzar was bent on fashioning loyal Babylonians from these vulnerable hostages.

Now we come to the first great challenge.

Daniel and his companions were ushered into the banquet hall of King Nebuchadnezzar. The great table was spread with a rich variety of Babylonian delicacies. Candlelight shimmered and danced off the golden bowls. The guests were seated and invited to partake.

That's when Daniel faced a choice. There were two problems with this food. First, it had been offered to idols. Daniel believed that to eat it would be to participate in the worship of those idols, something that he was continually being pressured to do. Second, according to God's clear instructions, much of the food was unclean; it was not to be eaten.

Staring at this tempting feast, Daniel must have felt a tremendous urge just to go along. The glories of Babylon dazzled his senses. The finest wines of the land beckoned him. Why keep hanging on to his religious scruples? Surely in this foreign culture he could wink at a few rules.

For a hostage who had seen the land of the true God desolated, it might have been very easy to cast his lot with the new power, the new dominant culture of Babylon. But this young captive made a remarkable decision. "Daniel resolved not to defile himself with the royal food and wine, and he asked the chief official for permission not to defile himself this way" (Daniel 1:8).

"Daniel resolved." What a story is contained in these words! Here is a decision that would reverberate through history. Its lessons would echo and reecho throughout the centuries. Daniel made his choice. He would be faithful to the Lord of heaven and earth—even as a hostage to another monarch. He would honor his God in the details of life—even while surrounded by a heathen culture. It might cost him his life, nevertheless he would be faithful to God.

Do you know what will help us survive as captives in an increasingly evil world? Do you know what will count in the end time? The example of Daniel. Remember: "Daniel resolved." He determined to be faithful to God long before the test at the banquet. He had made up his mind that he wasn't going to sell out in order to have it easy in Babylon. He was going to remain a child of the living God. He was not going to let this heathen culture take away his faith piece by piece.

That's how it usually happens. The enemy typically doesn't try to overwhelm us all at once. He just tries to chip away at our faith a little at a time. "This practice is not so important," he says. "You could live without that belief."

Friends, I think it boils down to this: People who flourish in the end time will be people who know who they are, people who are secure in their relationship with God. If Daniel had been embarrassed about his identity as a Hebrew, if he'd tried to hide his religious scruples, then he

probably would have given in to the pressure to conform—
and disappeared in Babylonian history.

But he was not embarrassed by his faith. Far from it.
Daniel was confident that his Lord knew best. Those who
survive at the end time will be those who know and love
God's truth. They would rather die than bring dishonor
to God.

When Daniel voiced his objections to the food at the
banquet, the official replied that he was worried about
what Nebuchadnezzar would say if the Hebrew hostages
didn't partake of the king's food. The official had taken a
liking to this noble young man, but he feared that Daniel
and his companions would start looking rather scrawny if
they didn't eat the delicacies spread before them.

Here's where Daniel showed his confidence. He made
the following proposal, recorded in Daniel 1:12, 13: " 'Please
test your servants for ten days: Give us nothing but vegetables to eat and water to drink. Then compare our appear-
ance with that of the young men who eat the royal food,
and treat your servants in accordance with what you see.' "

Daniel believed that the principles God had laid out in
Scripture were for the benefit of humanity. He was bold
enough to propose an experiment, a ten-day test. He and
his Hebrew friends would eat the simple Judean diet,
probably of fruits, nuts, grains, and vegetables. The others
would have the rich, spicy diet, heavy with meats.

This must have been the world's first comparative di-
etary study. And Scripture records the results. It says that
at the end of the ten days, the Hebrews "looked healthier
and better nourished than any of the young men who ate
the royal food" (verse 15).

And so Daniel was able to continue abiding by the
principles of God's Word; he continued being faithful in
the details. Why? Not because he had compromised, but
because he'd boldly issued a challenge. He offered to dem-

onstrate that God's way was best. He was confident in the principles of his faith.

That's the kind of godly boldness we need in the end times. Are you committed to God's truth? Are you convinced that there's no better way to live?

How is it in your life right now? Are there compromises? Are there areas in your life in which you are knowingly violating God's will? When someone makes a racist slur or an obscene joke, do you just go along? When you're offered a drink, or maybe some drugs, do you just try to conform? What are you feeding your mind with? You cannot develop spiritual thoughts if you feed your mind with the world's agenda.

Daniel was a hostage with a mission—not just to survive, but to be faithful to God. Daniel resolved. Daniel decided ahead of time. No matter where, no matter when, God's way is best.

Friends, in the time of the end, great pressure will be brought to bear on every man, woman, and child who attempts to serve the true God. Have you decided in your heart that the only thing that really matters is, not what other people think, but what God thinks? Have you resolved to be faithful to Him—unconditionally?

Daniel made that decision. For him, that decision turned disaster into triumph. The book of Daniel opens with a great disaster: the destruction of Jerusalem, the apparent defeat of God's people. But soon, through the faithfulness of a few Hebrews, we see a hint of God's triumph.

Listen to what happened when Daniel and his fellow Hebrew hostages were brought before Nebuchadnezzar. "The king talked with them, and he found none equal to Daniel, Hananiah, Mishael and Azariah; so they entered the king's service. In every matter of wisdom and understanding about which the king questioned them, he found them ten times better than all the magicians and enchanters in his whole kingdom" (verses 19, 20).

The four Hebrews were still held in Babylon. They were still surrounded by an alien culture. And they were called into the king's service. But here's the difference: they did not serve Nebuchadnezzar as Babylonians; they did not go in as idol worshipers. They went in as representatives of the God of heaven and earth, and as such they had a tremendous influence in that great kingdom. They retained the unique wisdom that has as its source the fear of God.

These men could never have been used for good if they'd started discarding their faith piece by piece. They would never have stood head and shoulders above all the "magicians and enchanters of the whole kingdom."

Daniel and his companions show us how to stand in the end time. They resolved to be faithful to God no matter what. They determined to choose God's principles over a secular culture. And they were confident that God's way is best.

Daniel chose not to indulge in the king's delicacies because he was looking forward to another banquet. The book of Revelation tells us about the marriage supper of the Lamb that will be celebrated when the redeemed are welcomed into heaven. All God's children will sit down with Him to a great feast. It will be like a family reunited at last, gathered around a table of love. That banquet is worth waiting for. It's worth being faithful for.

Will you determine in your heart to be there for the banquet—no matter what? Will you dare to be a Daniel?

It's so important to have a strong purpose, to be able to stand alone. Forces are building in our world that will soon bear down on all those who want to be loyal to God. We need to determine in our hearts now to be faithful to Him, to demonstrate that His way is best. And we can have confidence that He will make us Daniels; He will help us be overcomers instead of just conformers.

Satan's Final Strategy

The early autumn sun cast its first faint rays across Lake Michigan, beautifully silhouetting the sleeping city of Chicago. The glow of that soft dawning light cast an aura of peace and tranquility over the scene. No one suspected that soon a grisly real-life drama would take place here that would stun a whole nation.

It was Wednesday, October 5, 1982. Twelve-year-old Mary Kellerman awoke unusually early complaining of a sore throat and runny nose. Her parents gave her one extra-strength Tylenol capsule and encouraged her to rest. At 7:00 a.m. they found Mary dying on the bathroom floor.

Before the week ended, seven Chicago-area residents had died after consuming Tylenol—and more would follow. Drugstores and supermarkets from coast to coast pulled Tylenol packages from their shelves, triggering one of the biggest nationwide drug alerts in history.

No one had suspected the medication wasn't safe. No one dreamed that someone, somewhere, somehow had tampered with some capsules, lacing them with cyanide, a poison so deadly it kills within minutes.

People became wary of all "over-the-counter" medications. Everyone wondered how they could be sure the pills in some trusted name-brand bottle hadn't been contaminated. The capsule little Mary swallowed that fateful morning had looked and felt and tasted like all the others.

The Tylenol tragedy made us all aware of how vulnerable we really are. No one wanted to be deceived by some madman's hoax. We realized as never before that some deceptions are terribly fatal. But how could we know the facts? How could we be safe?

Pharmaceutical companies desperately tried to reassure consumers. They rushed "tamper-proof" containers on the market and promised to emphasize product safety.

But still, our world doesn't seem quite as safe as before, does it? Evil seems to strike with such random violence these days. A truck driver stops at a light in south-central Los Angeles and is beaten almost to death by young men enraged over a trial verdict in Simi Valley. A young Mexican boy is drinking milk at the kitchen table when a stray bullet ends his life—gang members shooting at one another.

No, the world isn't as safe as it used to be. And Bible prophecy indicates that it's not going to get any safer. The forces of evil are gathering for a final assault, and we know that evil isn't just something that happens on the streets. It also seeks to penetrate our lives. The poison tries to seep in. So we face an important question: Is there any way to "tamper-proof" our lives? Is there a way to resist deadly deceptions during the time of the end?

I believe there is. And I believe the first step is to understand the nature of the poison, the nature of the threat.

For centuries a worldwide hoax has been deceiving millions. Maybe even you! A fallen angel has been tampering with the pure teachings of God's Word—adulterating His truth with poisonous fallacies just as deadly as the tainted Tylenol capsules. And God has sounded a worldwide alert.

The Bible's last book, Revelation, reveals Satan's final, cleverly deceptive strategy. It's actually a strategy he's used before—to great effect. He used it to deceive one-third of the angels. He used it to deceive our first parents, Adam and Eve. He used it to deceive Israel, and he even tried it on Christ. Why has it been so effective?

Come back with me thousands of years to the epicenter of the universe. Here in the cosmic control room, the nerve center of God's government, a brilliant angel attempts a brilliant coup. He leads one-third of the angels in open, direct rebellion against God.

The exiled prophet John describes the scene in these words: "There was war in heaven. Michael and his angels fought against the dragon, and the dragon and his angels fought back. But he was not strong enough, and they lost their place in heaven. The great dragon . . . was hurled to the earth, and his angels with him" (Revelation 12:7-9).

Incredible as it may seem, the reason there is conflict on earth is because there was first conflict in heaven. Heaven's harmony was destroyed; its peace was broken up. Angels who'd been friends for centuries turned into bitter enemies. Battle lines were drawn sharply on those streets of gold. Every angel had to declare his loyalty. Seraphim and cherubim chose sides. There was no middle ground.

What led to this unthinkable war? What thought processes went on in the mind of Lucifer—that bright angel who would become Satan? How could he possibly deceive one-third of the heavenly host? How could beings so close to God fall for his lies?

These are questions that concern us a great deal as we face the end times. Jesus once warned His closest followers that false Christs and false prophets would arise just before His second coming. He stated that they would attempt to deceive even the elect.

Satan's supreme goal is to lead millions to accept his subtle deceptions at the end time. And he will use the strategy that has served him so well in the past. It seduced one-third of heaven's angels; why not use it again? If it produced rebellion in heaven, surely it will produce disaster on earth. To survive with your faith intact at the end of time, you must understand what Satan's strategy is all about. It's a matter of life and death.

Fortunately, the prophet Isaiah lifts the veil from Lucifer's mind and helps us understand his thought processes. Listen to what Isaiah says: "How you have fallen from heaven, O morning star, son of the dawn. . . . You said in your heart, 'I will ascend to heaven; I will raise my throne above the stars of God; I will sit enthroned on the mount of assembly, on the utmost heights of the sacred mountain. I will ascend above the tops of the clouds; I will make myself like the Most High' " (Isaiah 14:12-14).

Here, in the depths of Lucifer's mind, we begin to see the essence of his strategy. Lucifer, whose name means "light bearer," desired the worship due God alone. He had "I" trouble. He became the center of his own universe. Lucifer wanted to be served rather than serve. He wanted to issue orders rather than obey.

His real motive is unmasked in the expression, "I will exalt my throne." A throne implies rulership. It indicates kingly authority. Lucifer wanted to usurp the authority that belongs only to God.

That's why he went out to incite discontent among the angels. Submission to God had slowly become distasteful. And he tried to inject that same disobedient spirit into the thoughts of other heavenly beings. Lucifer had to be very subtle, of course. At first he simply raised questions about God's law. Was the law really necessary for angels? Was it fair for God to tell everyone how to live? Why shouldn't angels in heaven be able to do exactly as they pleased?

Lucifer contaminated the minds of angels with his own rebellious spirit by getting them to believe that obedience was unnecessary. Now we are at the heart of the enemy's time-tested, fatal deception. He maintains that the law of God is optional, that we don't have to submit to it.

That's the poison. That's the deception that has contaminated so much of our world today. And it's getting more and more deadly.

It has contaminated the family. You can see it in the faces of children whose fathers have abandoned them, fathers who think they've found freedom. You can hear it in the sobs of battered wives whose husbands come home drunk every Friday night.

You can see that deadly poison spread through society. We've come to assume that we can make up the rules as we go along, that we are responsible only to our "true selves." The result is an epidemic of addictions. AIDS cuts down more and more lives. Countless inner-city youths are lost to violence and despair.

Satan has been tampering with our world, using this fatal deception—"God's law is optional. Obedience is not really necessary." Even many churches have been contaminated. How many times have you heard believers say, "The only thing that matters is your relationship with Christ; there aren't any rules"?

Well, it's very true that our relationship with Christ is the only thing that matters. But it's equally true that a healthy relationship with Him involves submission and obedience. Christ is our moral teacher as well as our intimate friend. And too many Christians have stopped learning. They cry, "Jesus only," and become flippant regarding a radical discipleship that leads to obedience.

The first step in "tamper-proofing" our lives is to recognize Satan's lie and to take a stand against it. Obedience and submission to God's truth are important; they're a vital part of the relationship with Christ that will enable us to stand in the end. This becomes apparent when we look closely at how Christ Himself dealt with Satan's strategy.

Christ saw that Satan had directly challenged God's character by questioning His law. When Satan said the law was restrictive, he was actually picturing God as a harsh taskmaster. When he implied that the law was not designed for human happiness, he was portraying God as a being interested only in Himself.

But Christ knew that God's laws reveal eternal principles of happiness and fulfillment; they reveal the character of a loving heavenly Father who has our best interests in view.

This, then, became the crux of the conflict between Christ and Satan—the character of God. The questions to be settled were these: "Is God's way really best? Does obedience really produce happiness?"

God's answer was the most dramatic event in human history. God the Son took on the frailty of human flesh and dwelt among us! Jesus Christ lived out His days in complete submission to God the Father—and He produced a life of incredible abundance. Jesus demonstrated that a life of complete obedience would become the light of the whole world.

Listen to how Jesus expressed His deepest desire. John records His words: "My food . . . is to do the will of him who sent me and to finish his work" (John 4:34).

Christ's adversary, Satan, was not going to take this challenge lying down. He mobilized the forces of hell to destroy this rabbi from Nazareth who exulted in the will of the Father.

During Jesus' final hours, His adversary vented all the anger he'd accumulated through the centuries. Roman soldiers whipped and beat Him. Crowds jeered and mocked at Him. Officials insulted Him. A jagged crown of thorns was jammed down on His head. His limbs were spiked to a tree. A spear pierced His side.

But there was more than mere anger in Satan's final, vicious attacks. The enemy still had not given up on his fundamental strategy. He was trying to make Jesus give up in hopeless despair; he wanted Jesus to disobey His Father. The moment of truth came in the Garden of Gethsemane. The fate of the world hung in the balance. Would Jesus take on His shoulders the sins of humanity, the unbearable burden? Would He accept the agonizing sentence?

Jesus said yes. He would go all the way. He remained true to the fundamental philosophy of His life: "Not as I will, but as you will" (Matthew 26:39). Jesus would not allow anything to keep Him from submitting to the Father—even the prospect of hell.

And so the ordeal of the cross proved to be Christ's great triumph. He had answered the challenge of Satan's rebellion. He had demonstrated that obedience to God is not only necessary, it is also the best way for human beings to live. At the end of His life, unjustly condemned, violently abused, and sentenced to a cruel death, Christ revealed that deep inner peace comes from unswerving devotion to God.

Christ triumphed. And His triumph relates directly to how we can further "tamper-proof" our lives. We've already seen that we have to recognize the poison, recognize Satan's final strategy. But we also need to experience the alternative. Paying lip service to God's law is one thing. Actually living a life of obedience is quite another.

Here's what the victorious Christ does for us. Not only does He offer us forgiveness and right standing with God, He also offers to fill us with His Spirit; He empowers us so that we can begin to experience the joy of His triumphant life. Paul describes this process in detail in Romans, chapters 6, 7, and 8. In chapter 8, the apostle writes that God sent His Son "in order that the righteous requirements of the law might be fully met in us, who do not live according to the sinful nature but according to the Spirit" (verse 4).

This is God's great plan. The Spirit of Christ is the one who "tamper-proofs" our lives. As we drink in that Spirit of truth through daily meditation on God's Word, we are insulated from Satan's deceptions. The poison doesn't reach us because of God's healing balm within.

At the end of time God longs for a whole generation of followers who are so transformed, so fundamentally changed, that they love what He loves. They find in His law their highest delight. Did you know that the Bible's last book, Revelation, pictures such a people?

Revelation 12 describes Satan's final attack on God's people. It mentions the characteristics of those who successfully resist that final assault. Notice these compelling words: "Then the dragon was enraged at the woman and went off to make war against the rest of her offspring—those who obey God's commandments and hold to the testimony of Jesus" (verse 17). In the symbolic prophecies of Revelation, the dragon represents Satan. A pure, chaste woman represents the bride of Christ, or His church. In this passage of Scripture Satan is pictured as being furious with Christ's church. And He decides to make war against "the rest of her offspring," the remnant, or those believers living in the end of time.

Now carefully notice how these people are described. They "obey God's commandments." What is true now will be doubly true then; holding on to Jesus involves obeying God's commands.

Satan hates those who find delight in obedience, because they are living proof that he is dead wrong about God.

Christ triumphed over the rebellion of Satan with His righteous life. But we are also given a part in that triumph. In the time of the end it will be our privilege to bear witness to the justice and fairness of God. Our submission to God's will, our loyalty to His law, further exposes the falsehood of Satan's claims. We show that God's way is best.

You'll recall from the previous chapter that Daniel did precisely that in the courts of Babylon. He remained faithful to God in a hostile, heathen world and proved that there really is great blessing in obedience to the Most High.

Similarly, God will have His Daniels in the final hours of earth's history—a group of people who find their highest delight in doing His will. They have been given new hearts and have received the Spirit of the living Christ. They show that faithfulness to God is worth any cost.

Now all this is impossible for us on our own. We're naturally self-centered. We naturally go with the flow and bend with the wind. Our flawed human nature resists submitting to the divine will. God understands this. That's why He has already provided for us a great triumph in Christ.

The heroic life of Christ is a priceless gift, available to all in the time of the end. It is our pardon. It is our power. God's Spirit within enables us to experience the positive, abundant life of Jesus—even in the midst of chaos.

Perhaps you're a bit skeptical about all this. You may be wondering if God really can change your life so dramatically.

Let me tell you about something that happened to me while I was conducting a series of meetings in Moscow's Kremlin Congress Hall.

I was talking with my translator in a dressing room after the meeting one evening when the door suddenly burst open. A large Russian man rushed in. He talked loudly and gestured wildly with his hands. At first I thought something I'd said that evening in the auditorium had offended him. But finally my translator was able to relate his story.

His name was Sergei. For years he'd been in and out of Russian jails. He was a hardened criminal. He described the horrible squalor and filth in prison. And then Sergei blurted out the questions that were burning inside him.

"Sir, I am sorry for everything I've done," he said. "How can I be forgiven? How can I be free from the accusing voices inside? How can I become a law-abiding citizen, wanting to do right rather than wrong?"

This man was staring at what seemed to be insurmountable obstacles. The poison of the enemy had seeped deeply into his heart through a life of crime.

But I was able to point Sergei to Jesus, the One whose mercy is endless and whose love is wider than the ocean. And I was able to share my faith in the triumphant Christ, who can take away our stony hearts and give us new hearts of flesh and put His Spirit inside us.

Sergei listened attentively as I assured Him that coming to Jesus in faith brings forgiveness. In coming to Jesus we come in contact with the source of spiritual power.

Sergei and I knelt on the floor to pray. His body began to tremble. He'd never prayed before. But with quivering lips he reached out to God. "Lord, tonight I come to You," he said. "For years I've lived a life of total rebellion against You. Tonight I ask You to forgive me and change me inside. Help me to love to obey You. Amen."

As we got up from our knees, Sergei's eyes glistened with tears. He gently smiled. Looking me straight in the eye, he said quietly, "Pastor, thank you; I feel different inside now!"

In the days that followed it became evident that Sergei's life had changed. He had a sense of forgiveness; the past no longer haunted him. I'm sure he will struggle with habits, as we all do. But he has the triumphant Christ on his side now. And that makes all the difference.

What God did for Sergei, He can do for you. There's no sin so bad that He can't forgive it. There's no habit so strong that He can't break it. He can radically transform you. His truth is stronger than Satan's poison.

Faith
in the Flames

Going along with the crowd is something that comes naturally, almost instinctively. We want to be where the action is. And besides, how can all these people really be wrong? The pull is especially strong if it's a religious crowd.

But a time is coming soon when just going with the flow will become exceedingly dangerous. A time is coming soon when the crowd will go right over a cliff!

In this chapter we're going to go back in time to a remarkable scene on the plains of Dura near ancient Babylon. An enormous gold statue of King Nebuchadnezzar had been set up, and thousands of representatives from his empire were invited to pay homage to it in a splendid ceremony. But when the vast assembly on the plain bowed to the ground toward the image, three young men remained standing.

They had to go against the crowd—a solemn religious crowd. They must have been quite conspicuous, all alone, the only irreverent ones amid a unified multitude prostrating itself. But they had something that enabled them to stand against the crowd, something very special that will also stand us in good stead in the end times.

The three Hebrew young men were named Shadrach, Meshach, and Abednego. They'd been carried captive from Israel and were being trained to help govern the vast Babylonian Empire. The three were required to appear before this gold statue along with representatives of every nation and tribe under Nebuchadnezzar's control.

Suddenly, trumpets sounded, and the king's herald made an announcement in a loud voice that rang over the plain. He declared, "This is what you are commanded to do, O people, nations and men of every language: As soon as you hear the sound of the horn, flute, zither, lyre, harp, pipes and all kinds of music, you must fall down and worship the image of gold that King Nebuchadnezzar has set up. Whoever does not fall down and worship will immediately be thrown into a blazing furnace" (Daniel 3:4-6).

Nebuchadnezzar didn't just want loyal subjects, he wanted *total allegiance*, the kind that makes people fall down and worship. So the three Hebrews, who'd been taught since childhood that there was only one God worthy of man's worship, had to make a hard choice. Would they go along with everybody else? Would they bow down to a counterfeit image, violating the commandments of God?

That's an important question for us to consider in our day. It's important especially because this decree has a striking parallel with another decree found in the book of Revelation, chapter 13. This chapter talks about a challenge God's people will face at the end of time. It tells us that an antichrist power will set up an image to his representative, the beast. This beast, verse 15 tells us, was able to "cause all who refused to worship the image to be killed."

In Daniel and in Revelation, a world leader attempts to compel worship to an image by issuing a decree. In both cases this decree requires something that contradicts a specific commandment of God and demands the death of all who do not submit. To whom are we going to bow down? That's the ultimate question.

At some point, believers are going to be confronted by a great power, a religious and political power, which demands their ultimate allegiance. How will we survive during that time? Let's return to those three Hebrews on the plains of Dura.

When the royal orchestra struck up its fanfare to King Nebuchadnezzar, everyone bowed on cue. Everyone except Shadrach, Meshach, and Abednego; they simply would not bow to this idol.

The king was outraged, of course, that anyone would interrupt his moment of glory. He had the three men brought before him. But when he saw that they were the friends of Daniel, men whom he'd come to respect and like, he decided to give them another chance to bow.

Nebuchadnezzar pointed to the blazing furnaces that had been prepared for any who might make trouble. He knew that the young men had an allegiance to their own God, but he asked, very pointedly, "What god will be able to rescue you from my hand?"

The answer these Hebrew youth gave is justly famous. "O Nebuchadnezzar, we do not need to defend ourselves before you in this matter. If we are thrown into the blazing furnace, the God we serve is able to save us from it, and he will rescue us from your hand, O king. But even if he does not, we want you to know, O king, that we will not serve your gods or worship the image of gold you have set up" (Daniel 3:16-18). These men answered the proud king's challenge without hesitation. They did so by testifying of their faith in the God of heaven and earth.

Yes, He could deliver them from the furnace, no matter how hot Nebuchadnezzar might make it. Their God was sovereign over all; He could do anything. That was the kind of God they served.

I believe we get a picture here of the kind of faith that will bring us through the end time—whatever those days may be like. These Hebrews had their eyes fixed on how great God is, not on how hot the furnace was. When pressured, they didn't try to make excuses or squirm out of a tight spot; they took the opportunity to testify of God's power.

And they did something else. They talked about their commitment to Him. "Even if He chooses *not* to deliver us," they vowed, "we will still not betray Him; we will still worship Him and Him alone."

A weak faith won't get us through the rough times in life, and a weak faith certainly won't stand in the end times. If our faith depends on God always giving us what we want, on things going smoothly, then we have our eyes fixed on the wrong things.

Real faith is a relationship with God based on a belief that He knows what is best for us—period. It involves a commitment to do what God asks—regardless of the consequences.

Let me tell you about one man who met adversity in the way these three Hebrews did, by testifying of his faith.

Two men confronted each other in a Romanian prison around 1950. One was a self-assured, intelligent, tough young lieutenant named Grecu. He was a dedicated Communist who thought he was making a better world.

The other individual was a young Lutheran pastor named Richard Wurmbrand. He was weak and pale. On his face were the heavy shadows of a man who has endured torture and deprivation.

Grecu sat at a desk with a rubber truncheon in his hand. He had been interrogating the pastor. On this morning, he shouted, "Your story was lies." He was angry that the pastor had not given him the names of his associates and of his connections with the West.

Grecu pushed back his chair and shouted, "Enough! Here's some paper. We know you've been communicating in code with other prisoners. Now we must know exactly what each of them said." The lieutenant cracked the truncheon on his desk, said, "You have half an hour!" and stomped out of the room.

Richard Wurmbrand faced a terrible dilemma as he stared at that white piece of paper. He had to write a confession. Yet he didn't want to reveal anything that might endanger his fellow prisoners. Almost anything he said could be twisted and turned into evidence that he was a spy.

Finally, this pastor decided to make a confession—of his faith in Jesus Christ. He admitted that he had been tapping in code on the cell walls, trying to communicate the good news about a Saviour.

He also testified in these words: "I am a disciple of Christ who has given us love for our enemies. I have never spoken against the Communists. I understand them and pray for their conversion, so that they will become my brothers in the faith."

Lieutenant Grecu returned after half an hour, swinging his truncheon; he'd been beating prisoners. He picked up the paper and began to read. After a while he put his truncheon aside.

When he came to the end of the pastor's confession, he looked up with troubled eyes and said, "Mr. Wurmbrand, why do you say you love me? This is one of your Christian commandments that no one can keep. I couldn't love someone who shut me up for years alone, who starved and beat me."

The pastor replied, "It's not a matter of keeping a commandment. When I became a Christian, it was as if I had been reborn, with a new character that was full of love."

For two hours these men talked earnestly about Christianity and Marxism. This young pastor took a stand in that prison of terror. He resisted—by a positive confession and by proclaiming what he did believe.

Those three Hebrews also wanted to proclaim what they believed. It wasn't enough for them just to refuse to bow to an idol; they must powerfully testify of their faith and confidence in God.

And what was the result? Well, an enraged Nebuchadnezzar had his furnaces heated to the maximum and had the Hebrews thrown into the flames.

I think again of the decree of the antichrist in Revelation who demands that everyone conform on pain of death. A fiery trial is coming to our world greater than any we have ever experienced in history. God's people will go through a crisis over the issue of the commandments of God.

But here's the important point: that final crisis need not terrify us. It can be an opportunity for us to see our Lord, very close and very powerful. Do you know what those Hebrews found in that furnace? They found none other than the Lord Jesus Christ. He was already there in the flames; He was standing with them. In the flames of life, Christ is there!

Nebuchadnezzar was astounded to see four men *walking* around in those flames. And the fourth man was "like the Son of God" (Daniel 3:25, KJV).

These young Hebrews had their eyes fixed on a great God, and in their hour of trial they found that a great God had come to be with them. That's what an unconditional faith, a committed faith, can do for us. It will bring God close in the worst of times.

Let me tell you about a remarkable man who exhibited this kind of faith.

On one of his many journeys through the Himalayas, the Indian evangelist Sundhar Singh discovered a Tibetan preacher whom the people treated with superstitious reverence. He could proclaim Christ without fear of reprisal, even though other preachers were violently persecuted. The preacher told Singh his story.

He'd once been secretary to a Buddhist priest but then

had come under the influence of a Christian from India. Eventually, he declared himself a follower of Jesus. He first confessed his faith to his own master, the Buddhist priest.

Within a few days, the preacher was sentenced to death. In front of the temple walls men bound a wet yak skin around him and sewed it up tight. Then they left him out in the scorching sunshine, where the contracting skin would crush him to death.

He did not die quickly enough, so red-hot skewers were thrust through the yak skin into his body. Later they tore off the skin and dragged him through the streets to a refuse dump outside of town. After further abuse, the preacher was dropped on a dunghill. His body showed no signs of life. The crowds left, and the vultures gathered.

But this mutilated victim was still alive. Somehow he managed to crawl away and recover. Then, instead of fleeing for his life, he marched right back into the village and began preaching about Christ! He could still testify about his faith; he could speak of a great God who had come close. The people now listened in awe.

Those three Hebrews in the fiery furnace also made a life-changing impact on haughty King Nebuchadnezzar. He rushed up to the edge of the furnace and called them out. As they emerged, a large crowd gathered around. They noticed that the Hebrews' hair wasn't even singed; their robes were not scorched; they didn't even carry the smell of smoke! Ultimately that fiery trial burned only one thing—the ropes that bound them. It freed them from their bonds. Shadrach, Meshach, and Abednego came out con-querors.

The trials of life can either make you bitter or make you better. They can either strengthen your faith or destroy it. The difference is whether you focus upon the Christ or the crisis.

Through your tears, heartaches, and disappointments you can see Christ. He is there in the flames of your life.

Possibly your life has been torn apart by divorce. You may be going through a very painful family problem right now. Possibly you have severe health problems or you may be facing serious financial difficulties. In the flames of life, He is there. Look through your tears. The understanding, compassionate Christ is there by your side to whisper words of encouragement.

Nebuchadnezzar now realized that there was a God in heaven far bigger than he could ever be. He called the three Hebrews "servants of the Most High God" (verse 26). Up to this point the king had tried to be the most high himself, with his massive golden statue. But now he made a remarkable confession. We find it in Daniel 3:28. "Praise be to the God of Shadrach, Meshach and Abednego, who has sent his angel and rescued his servants! They trusted in him and defied the king's command and were willing to give up their lives rather than serve or worship any god except their own God."

Nebuchadnezzar's rage had turned to admiration. The unconditional faith of the Hebrews had proved contagious. It's confessing our faith when times get hard that really has an impact. The faith that will stand in the end time is also the faith that will win others in the end time.

Richard Wurmbrand, the pastor I told you about earlier who made his confession of faith, had quite an impact on Lieutenant Grecu. After that first long talk, the lieutenant invited him back to his office almost every day, and they would talk for at least an hour.

Pastor Wurmbrand told him that the early believers were actually part of a revolutionary movement. Grecu was surprised to learn that Karl Marx had once written that Christianity is "the ideal religion for the renewal of lives made wretched by sin."

As they continued to talk, Grecu was more and more impressed by the Christian ideals of love and service to everyone. Frequently he would say, "I was brought up an atheist, and I'll never be anything else." But this pastor standing before him was an argument he could not refute. God was real.

Two weeks after they'd begun their dialogue, Lieutenant Grecu realized he had come to love Jesus and decided to receive Christ as his Saviour. What a scene it was there in the prison as the lieutenant in his security police uniform knelt beside Pastor Wurmbrand in his patched prison rags. The lieutenant made his prayer of confession, and when they rose to their feet, the two men were brothers.

There's nothing quite as eloquent as faith under fire. Wouldn't you like to have a faith like that? A totally committed faith? A faith that will stand tall when times get rough? It's available to each of us.

God wants to develop this strong faith in you! Faith is developed as we make Jesus and His Word the center of our lives. If you will spend time with God, quality time communicating with Him, a committed faith will result. If you will spend time looking at Jesus as your Saviour and Lord, an unyielding faith will result.

Let's decide ahead of time that we'll develop a relationship with God based on real trust. Let's trust that He knows best, no matter what. Let's trust that He will see us through the end times.

It's really rather simple. The three Hebrews didn't bow to the golden image, because they were already bowing to someone else. We know that times are coming when harsh decrees will be passed. Minds will be manipulated, and false worship enforced. But we also know that our Lord can make us loyal and courageous and true. Pray that He will build that trust in you in the midst of your conflicts day by day.

The Footsteps
of the Beast

As my KLM flight headed from Moscow to Amsterdam at 33,000 feet, I discovered that my seatmate on the plane had been one of President Jimmy Carter's political advisers on Soviet affairs. We began talking about the dramatic changes sweeping through Eastern Europe, and I decided to ask him a question.

"Let's suppose," I said, "that I'm the president and you are advising me. How would you describe the future of the former Soviet Union?"

My companion responded thoughtfully, "I see the future described in two words—fragmentation and chaos."

If you've glanced at a newspaper or switched on the TV news lately, you're probably aware that the two words this gentleman used could be applied to quite a few places in our world today. Even though we're all trying to breathe a great big sigh of relief because the Cold War is over, it's pretty hard to celebrate. Conflicts seem to be multiplying.

In Yugoslavia the collapse of Communism laid bare an age-old animosity between the Serbs and Croatians. No one seems able to stop the slaughter of civilians there. Factional leaders keep speaking of peace while partisans keep filling villages with bullet holes.

Some observers fear that the entire Baltic region could explode in ethnic conflicts just as it did before the First World War.

Many of the countries that have broken off from the former Soviet Union face the same peril: Armenians fighting Muslims around Uzbekistan. Border wars. Ethnic rivalries. Power struggles.

A few years ago, after the fall of several dictatorships, it seemed that democracy would become the new watchword. But the new democracies remain frightfully unstable.

Recently citizens of Bangkok, Thailand, poured into the streets to protest widespread corruption in that country. But the protest turned into bloody rioting that seems to have encouraged the military to take a stronger hand.

The latest presidential elections in the Philippines were almost as unsettling. Scores of candidates fragmented the voters and compounded the usual name calling and slogan throwing. Straining under intense economic burdens, this country teeters on the edge of chaos.

It's just not a very reassuring picture out there. And we haven't even mentioned the hot spots that *never* seem to cool down: ancient religious hatreds in Northern Ireland. Ancient animosities in the struggle of Palestinian and Jew in Israel.

What we see around us is lawlessness on a grand scale. Over and over people resort to rifles and mortar rounds to resolve differences.

Nor is the prosperous West immune. Neo-Nazis and other fiercely nationalist movements have sprung up all over Europe, zealously trying to give intolerance and hatred a good name.

In the United States a sense of outrage over a trial verdict erupted in the Los Angeles riots. The fires and beatings were terrifying to watch. But they were only the most dramatic signs of a whole culture of lawlessness that has penetrated inner cities all over the country.

My seatmate on that KLM flight put it well—"fragmentation and chaos." Somehow the glue that keeps us together, that makes us adhere to the framework of law and order, is dissolving.

Listen carefully to a prediction Jesus once made. Talking about signs that indicate the end of the age, the time of the end, He gave us this general picture of the world situation. "Nations will be in anguish and perplexity at the roaring and tossing of the sea. Men will faint from terror, apprehensive of what is coming on the world" (Luke 21:25, 26).

The sea, in prophetic literature, often is a symbol for people and populations. Bible writers also used it to symbolize the realm of chaos, the place of disorder and evil. I believe these words of Jesus picture a time strikingly like our own, in which instability causes anguish and perplexity among governments everywhere. And we can only ask apprehensively, "What's coming next on the world?"

We're already beginning to see what's coming next. There's a reaction to this global plague of lawlessness. The pendulum has begun to swing the other way. Even as much of our world faces increasing fragmentation, great efforts are being made to unite and consolidate.

Following the dramatic success of an allied force in the liberation of Kuwait, President Bush spoke enthusiastically of the dawning of a new age in international politics. He saw a "new world order" coming over the horizon, a world order in which law and cooperation would replace chaos and conflict.

The European Common Market seemed headed toward a dead end a few years ago, but it's now going strong. Plans are well underway to introduce a common currency for all member nations so they can become a single economic force.

The United Nations also seems to have found its second wind. It has been successful in isolating countries that sponsor terrorism and in imposing embargoes on those who prey on their neighbors.

Instead of the major powers engaged in endless confrontations in the United Nations, we now see them working to build a consensus on a wide range of issues.

The conference on the environment at Rio de Janeiro may not have seemed a great triumph for environmentalists. But it was the first time the nations of the world had agreed to recognize the problems that threaten Mother Earth; they acknowledged that we have to unite and work together to fight global warming and the destruction of rain forests.

That's the bottom line for many world leaders today: we have to unite if we are ever going to deal with our overwhelming problems. We have to submit to a common order, a common law.

We've seen that Jesus predicted widespread instability as a sign of the end of the age and His return. What about this movement toward a new world order? Does that fit into the prophetic picture?

The aged apostle, John, writes with penetrating insight describing our day. He foretells a federation of nations just before the enforcement of the mark of the beast. "The ten horns you saw are ten kings who have not yet received a kingdom, but who for one hour will receive authority as kings along with the beast. They have one purpose and will give their power and authority to the beast" (Revelation 17:12, 13).

Interestingly enough, the book of Revelation tells us that at the time of the end a great power will attempt to enforce law and order in the name of world peace. This power, called "the beast," is introduced in Revelation 13. "And I saw a beast coming out of the sea. He had ten horns and seven heads . . . and on each head a blasphemous name. . . . The whole world was astonished and followed the beast" (verses 1, 3).

A beast in Bible prophecy represents a kingdom. It may be purely a civil power or a religious political power. This beast wears many crowns, has great authority and power, and possesses a throne. It blasphemes God and makes war against the people of God. Scholars are quite sure about what power was on the apostle John's mind as he wrote of this dragon.

He was referring to the pagan Roman Empire. It had devoured many kingdoms and thus wore many crowns. It was one of the most powerful empires that had ever existed. Its cult of emperor worship was regarded by believers as blasphemy against God. And it fiercely persecuted the early church.

Pagan Rome acted very much like a dragon to those who had pledged their allegiance to Jesus Christ. Revelation 12 identifies the dragon-like beast as Satan, or the devil (see verse 9). It is no surprise, though, that the devil works through earthly powers. Through whom was he working in chapter 12? The answer is clear. Revelation 12, verses 4 and 5, describe Herod's attempt to destroy the "manchild," Christ, as soon as He was born. Working through pagan Rome, Satan attempted to destroy Jesus.

In Revelation 13, a new beast arises, receiving its power from pagan Rome. There is much more to this new power, pictured in Revelation 13, than just the ancient Roman Empire. Verses 3 and 4 portray a worldwide system of worship. "The whole world was astonished and followed the beast. Men . . . worshiped the beast." The setting of Revelation 13 is true and false worship. The issues are clear. The beast usurps God's authority. It changes God's law. It enforces its own sign of allegiance.

This religious political system received the seat of its government from pagan Rome. Springing up out of Rome, it substituted the teachings of religious leaders for the Word of God. In this system tradition stands in the place of Scripture. Man's word replaces God's Word.

In a time of fragmentation, political crisis, and international chaos, a powerful worldwide religio-political leader will present himself as the one to unify the nations.

Now I'm sure you're beginning to see how ominous this "new world order" sounds in the light of prophecy. Times are desperate, political systems are falling apart, so people turn to some great power that can pull us all together. But what Revelation 13 tells us is that the person or organization who attempts to legislate law and order in the name of world peace will eventually roar like a beast.

Revelation 13:16, 17 tell us what the beast does: "He . . . forced everyone, small and great, . . . to receive a mark on his right hand or on his forehead, so that no one could buy or sell unless he had the mark."

You see here the pressure to conform to the new system. "If economies are in chaos," the argument goes, "then radical solutions are necessary. So get with the program, receive the mark of the beast, or get left out of the economy."

That pressure will turn into outright persecution, according to Revelation 13. Eventually the beast power issues a decree demanding that everyone who refuses to worship it be put to death. Tragically, those who have given it their allegiance will realize too late that they've become part of a monstrous system.

This then is the danger that lies ahead. We must beware of any power that attempts to unite political and religious authority and rule over the nations of the world.

But fortunately, the book of Revelation doesn't just talk about the danger, the problem. It also presents God's solution. In this book I don't want to just look at what's ahead; I also want to look at how to live confidently amid chaos in the time of the end!

In the last chapter we saw how three young Hebrews stood tall while facing a tyrant's decree to worship a great image. They showed us what unconditional, committed faith is all about. We need that same kind of faith in the end time. But in what, exactly, should we place such a faith? As we begin to hear the roar of the beast, what is it, specifically, about God that we need to focus on closely?

Revelation 14 gives us God's dramatic response to the beast's blasphemous challenge. It's the Almighty's final message of warning, and it's given by three angels flying over the earth who have an eternal gospel to proclaim. This is what they say: " 'Fear God and give him glory, because the hour of his judgment has come. Worship him who made the heavens, the earth, the sea and the springs of water' " (Revelation 14:7).

Who is it that stands against the roar of the beast? The Creator of heaven and earth. The One who breathes life into every creature. Only our Creator has the right to judge us; we are responsible to Him and Him alone.

The angels of Revelation 14 go on to warn about the terrible fate of those who worship the beast. And they tell us that this evil power is fallen, defeated.

Worshiping the beast is deadly. So how do we stand against it when pressured to conform? By fixing an unconditional faith on our Creator. He is bigger than the beast. The One who orchestrates the movements of the constellations and calls each star by name—His authority and power must overwhelm all others. Give Him glory; give Him allegiance; don't be deceived by the dazzling promises of the beast.

May I give you a very practical suggestion? There is actually a way for you to express your unconditional allegiance to the Creator regularly every week. It's found in the fourth commandment. Yes, the commandment about keeping the Sabbath holy, found in Exodus 20:8-11.

Do you recall *why* the commandment urges us to observe the seventh day, the Sabbath? That commandment tells us to remember the Sabbath because God created the world in six days and rested on the seventh. It reminds us that the Lord made "the heavens and the earth, the sea, and all that is in them" (verse 11), language very similar to that in this final warning in Revelation 14.

The Sabbath, then, is a symbol of our love and loyalty to our Creator. We observe the Sabbath as a way of keeping alive that bond with Him, renewing it each week. May I suggest that this can be a wonderful way to give God the Creator glory in the midst of chaos, while threatened by a roaring beast? It can help us to stand firm; it gives us a place to stand, when all the world seems to be following after a counterfeit authority.

A man named Polycarp made a very eloquent stand in the second century A.D. He was the bishop of Smyrna, a man who had to confront the blasphemous power of pagan Rome. Polycarp refused to go along with the cult of emperor worship; he would not divide his allegiance. And so he was brought to the arena in Smyrna, where a bloodthirsty crowd waited.

The proconsul there decided to try a little gentle persuasion first. "Respect your years!" he urged. "Swear by Caesar's fortune . . . say, 'Away with the atheists.' "

The Romans, with their countless gods, regarded the followers of Jesus as virtual atheists because they believed only in one God. The proconsul was actually trying to get Polycarp to say, "Away with the Christians."

But instead, the old man looked around at the chanting crowd in that stadium. He could hear the roar of the beast in their voices. And waving his hand toward *them*, he said, "Away with the atheists!"

The Roman official persisted, "Swear, and I will set you free; execrate Christ."

Polycarp answered him by declaring his unconditional faith. "For eighty-six years I have been His servant," the aged Christian said, "and He has never done me wrong. How can I blaspheme the king who saved me?"

As the crowd grew more restless, the official shouted, "I'll have you destroyed by fire unless you change."

Polycarp's reply showed that he was well aware of the fate of those who give their allegiance to the beast. He said, "The fire you threaten burns for a time and is soon extinguished. There is a fire you know nothing about—the fire of the judgment to come . . . reserved for the ungodly."

At this the proconsul gave up and announced that Polycarp had confessed to being a Christian. Immediately the crowd shouted that he be burned alive.

Polycarp removed his outer clothing, stood calmly by the pyre, and said a final prayer. His words show clearly what he was looking at in that cruel arena, surrounded by the roar of the beast.

He began, "O Father of thy beloved . . . Son, Jesus Christ, through whom we have come to know Thee, the God of angels and powers and all creation, and of the whole family of the righteous who live in Thy presence."

Polycarp fixed his eye of faith firmly on the Creator, the Lord of heaven and earth. There was room for no other allegiance. He would give this God the glory and no one else—no matter how loudly and persistently another power might call. And he was still looking in that direction when the flames leaped up over him.

Soon, I believe, we will be hearing the roar of the last beast, the final persecuting power. Soon we will need to declare our allegiance. If our faith is not fixed on the Creator, if our relationship with Him is not the highest priority in our lives, then those other voices will prove overwhelming.

But if we do give our unconditional allegiance to the one who created us and redeemed us, then we don't have to fear. The most timid among us will be given the boldness of Polycarp. We *will* be able to stand, because our God is able to make us stand.

Surviving
the Lion's Roar

It's one thing to hear the roar of danger off in the distance or far in the future. It's one thing to make promises to God in a safe and calm here and now.

But what if that roar suddenly erupted in your face, right now? What if your faith was tested by the fiery gaze of a lion? Would you be able to stand fast?

I'd like to tell you about a man who stood very much alone in a time of widespread corruption, a man who *was* tested by the roar of danger—up close. His career took him to the courts of the Medo-Persian Empire, during the reign of King Darius. The man—Daniel, the Old Testament's prophet of the end time.

Daniel had been taken captive by the Babylonians after the fall of Jerusalem and eventually rose to a position of trust under King Nebuchadnezzar. His unique character is demonstrated by this remarkable fact: Daniel survived the fall of one empire and its replacement by another. He served both the Babylonian king and the Persian monarch who conquered Babylon. Not many people are valued enough to make that kind of transition.

In the kingdom of Medo-Persia, Daniel became what we would call the first vice-president. The sixth chapter of Daniel tells us: "It pleased Darius to appoint 120 satraps [princes] to rule throughout the kingdom, with three administrators over them, one of whom was Daniel. The satraps were made accountable to them so that the king might not suffer loss. Now Daniel so distinguished himself among the administrators and satraps by his exceptional qualities that the king planned to set him over the whole kingdom" (verses 1-3).

Notice that Darius made his 120 bureaucrats accountable to the administrators "so that he might not suffer loss." Bribery, extortion, and fraud were as much a problem in the ancient world as they are now. Many of the officials who had managed to occupy positions of influence were interested only in furthering their own careers. They tended to pocket a good portion of whatever tax money passed through their hands. And they often enriched themselves at the expense of the king by keeping false financial records.

Daniel's responsibility was to see that the books were kept honestly. He was supposed to deal with corruption in the court. And apparently he did a very good job, because he distinguished himself by his integrity. And so Darius wanted to entrust "the whole kingdom" into this man's hands. Daniel was on his way to becoming the second most powerful man in the Medo-Persian Empire.

But not everyone was pleased by this. Some very much wanted to keep the status quo; they wanted to keep enriching themselves with government funds. And this strange Hebrew, who didn't fit in, the man always intent on straightening things out, was now going to be elevated in a position over them.

They just couldn't let that happen. So they huddled together in the Persian equivalent of a smoke-filled room and planned strategy. How could they move Daniel out of the picture? Darius trusted him implicitly. Why not find grounds for charges against him in his handling of government affairs?

These officials set about digging for dirt. They dug long and hard—and came up empty. Not a hint of corruption;

not even a trace of negligence. Daniel was not the kind of man who wears religion like a cloak that he can take off when circumstances seem to require it. Daniel's faith went to the bone.

"That's it!" someone realized. "His faith!" Daniel's enemies concluded: " 'We will never find any basis for charges against this man Daniel unless it has something to do with the law of his God' " (Daniel 6:5).

Daniel could not be bought off; he could not be blackmailed. There was only one way to get rid of him, and that was to enact a law that would put Daniel in the position of disobeying his God.

It's interesting to note that Daniel's enemies decided to attack him through "the law of his God." Specifically in this case, they decided to test him regarding the commandment to worship God—and God alone.

One day, the conspirators presented King Darius with a very flattering proposal. " 'O King Darius, live forever!' they said. 'The royal administrators, prefects, satraps, advisers and governors have all agreed that the king should issue an edict and enforce the decree that anyone who prays to any god or man during the next thirty days, except to you, O king, should be thrown into the lions' den' " (Daniel 6:6, 7).

These men suggested a sort of "King Darius Month"— a thirty-day period in which everyone would honor the monarch exclusively. Naturally, Darius took a liking to the idea. Such spontaneous devotion from his chief administrators! That was nice to hear after all his problems with their dishonesty. So he signed the decree into law, an irrevocable law that carried the death penalty.

The trap was set. Sooner or later Daniel was bound to fall into it. They would catch him worshiping his own God during the next thirty days and bring the king's decree down on his head.

Think about that for a moment. What if the simple act of prayer became a criminal offense? It might seem a simple, easy act to worship the God of heaven and earth in the privacy of your home. But what if praying meant that you might be put to death? What if worshiping the true God meant staring into the face of a lion? That sort of changes the picture, doesn't it?

The decree enacted by King Darius is similar to another ominous decree we find in the book of Revelation. Revelation 13 tells us about a decree the antichrist creates that forces all, small and great, rich and poor, to worship the image of the beast. Those who refuse are to be put to death.

Here we see a world power trying to force men and women to disobey a command of God about worship. That is the test coming on us. That is part of Satan's final strategy. How do we meet it? How can we have confidence that we'll stand in the end? Let's get back to Daniel's story.

"Now when Daniel learned that the decree had been published, he went home to his upstairs room where the windows opened toward Jerusalem. Three times a day he got down on his knees and prayed, giving thanks to his God, just as he had done before" (Daniel 6:10).

What a remarkable act of devotion!

Daniel could have tried to hide his religion. He could have tried to go along with the decree. Surely God would understand if he took a break from his worship routine. After all, he'd been so faithful before.

But now, he prayed toward Jerusalem, by the window, "just as he had done before." There's a beautiful testimony of courage in that simple act. Decree or no decree, Daniel was going to give his ultimate allegiance to the God of heaven and earth.

There's something else that impresses me about Daniel's prayer. He wasn't in a panic, begging God for a way out of his dilemma. His wasn't a desperate prayer. It was a prayer of thanksgiving! That's what the Bible says. Daniel was "giving thanks to his God" as was his custom.

This tells me something about this man's faith. It shows me why it stood the test during a time of crisis. Daniel treasured his relationship with his Lord; it was the most important thing in his life. He was thankful for the privilege of communicating with the Almighty. That was worth any price.

You know, a religion of convenience isn't going to make it in the last days when deadly decrees start coming our way. Religion as a once-a-week supplement to our lives isn't going to make it. Only a relationship with God that we value above all else is going to stand.

Like Daniel, the great reformer, John Hus, also based his life on obedience to his Lord. When Hus was condemned to the stake, he had to undergo what was called "the ceremony of degradation." Church dignitaries at the scene publicly stripped away his identity as a priest and as a Christian.

First, the cup of communion was taken from his hands, and the dignitaries denounced Hus. He responded by saying, "I hope to drink from the cup in the kingdom of God."

Next, the officials removed his garments one by one, pronouncing in each instance the appropriate curse. Hus replied that he was quite willing to suffer shame for the name of the Lord.

Finally, a tall, paper crown was placed on his head. On it was a picture of three devils fighting for possession of a soul and the inscription: "This is an arch-heretic." The bishops intoned a final curse, "We commit your soul to the devil!"

John Hus calmly replied, "And I commit it to the most merciful Lord Jesus Christ."

This courageous man was saying in effect: "You can take everything away from me; you can degrade me publicly, but you can't take away the most precious thing in life:

My relationship with the Lord Jesus Christ."

And that's the kind of testimony that Daniel made. Even under threat of certain death in the lions' den, he still cherished communion with his Lord. He would not betray that relationship.

Well, needless to say, Daniel's enemies spotted him praying and rushed into court with the news that someone was not celebrating "King Darius Month" properly. When the king learned who it was, he was dismayed. He realized he'd been tricked into signing the death warrant of the one man in his empire whom he trusted completely. But his hands were tied; the law could not be revoked.

Let's read what happened next. "They brought Daniel and threw him into the lions' den. The king said to Daniel, 'May your God, whom you serve continually, rescue you!' A stone was brought and placed over the mouth of the den" (Daniel 6:16, 17).

Now, let me ask you: How would you feel if you were thrown to the lions and told, "I hope your God rescues you somehow"?

That might not be much of a comfort to any of us. The stone lowered into place overhead, sealing us in with those hungry beasts, would appear to seal our fate. Not too many of us could spend a restful night with ravenous lions hanging around.

But here's the fascinating thing. King Darius was the one who tossed and turned all night in his palace. He couldn't eat a bite. That's what Scripture tells us. Darius was filled with guilt and anguish over what had happened. But Daniel had a nice, quiet evening in the company of the lions. He probably fell fast asleep with his head against one of the big cats.

How could he do that? Daniel could face the lions because he had his mind fixed on God, the God who can give us peace in the midst of terrible circumstances. But even more importantly, Daniel trusted God. And the result? The next morning, Daniel told Darius, "My God sent his angel, and he shut the mouths of the lions" (verse 22).

Daniel believed in a God who is sovereign over all, sovereign over history. He would turn the captivity of Israel into a blessing. Sovereign over individual lives. He had saved Daniel's three friends from the fiery furnace and used them as His witnesses in a heathen land. Sovereign over every situation. God could tame the lions in the darkness of that den.

Remember, the angel who came down to shut the lions' mouths was coming from the Creator, the One who had made these magnificent creatures in the first place. He was their master. With the Creator's authority, that angel could have asked the lions to do just about anything.

Those ravenous beasts became as gentle and friendly as overgrown house pets. God took care of His man in a time of crisis. And we have a promise of the same kind of protection in the final crisis. In Matthew 24, where Christ talks about the great tribulation that will precede His second coming, we find these words: "If those days had not been cut short, no one would survive, but for the sake of the elect those days will be shortened" (verse 22).

Now, often these verses are taken as a terrifying hint of a time that will be all but unbearable. But I don't think that's the main point. "Those days *will* be shortened." That's the important fact, I believe. God's chosen, His children, *will* make it through; we will be able to stand. We'll be safe even though surrounded by lions.

One cold winter day toward the end of World War II, an elderly woman walked out of what had seemed even worse than a lions' den. She was leaving the Ravensbruck concentration camp, where countless human beings had been systematically starved and worked to death. As the heavy iron gates closed behind her, Corrie ten Boom could hardly believe that she was alive—and free.

Corrie had been arrested by the Nazis for hiding Jews in her home in Holland. She and her family believed in a God who gives refuge to all, and they committed themselves to this dangerous work.

This quiet matron in her fifties had not imagined she could survive the horrors of a labor camp. But God had sustained her during the ordeal. Corrie saw many women brutalized at Ravensbruck; many perished, including her dear sister, Betsy. But many of those women died with the name of Jesus on their lips because of the witness of those two sisters. "Those women," Corrie wrote, "were well worth all our suffering."

Finally, as a result of what turned out to be a clerical error, Corrie was released. One week later, all the women her age at Ravensbruck were gassed.

As she walked out of this lions' den, this place of unspeakable suffering, Corrie had learned something invaluable. This is the testimony she would give, all over the world: "There is no place on earth so dark, so deep, that God's love is not deeper still."

Yes, Daniel discovered that God's love is deep enough to penetrate the stone sealing the lions' den. He found his God to be a very present help in trouble—because Daniel had always been very present with his Lord.

That's all that will matter during the earth's final crisis. Church structures will have crumbled. Seminars and books and retreats will disappear. Some of those closest to us may fall away. The only thing that will stand in that time of trouble is our individual, personal relationship with the Lord Jesus Christ. That's all we'll have.

But let me assure you, that will be more than enough.

Satan, that great dragon, Satan the roaring lion, will do his best to destroy God's people in the end. He will try to intimidate believers. But our God will shut the mouth of that ravenous lion. Satan will be bound. Angels will be sent to stand guard around us. That's how we'll survive the great tribulation. That's how we will find ourselves some-day in another time and another place, safe in the arms of our Father. We can look forward to the place where the lion and lamb will lie down together, where all animosities will cease, where the long history of people hurting each other will at last come to a close in the reign of Christ.

You can make it! You can be there! Just remember that the same Lord who delivered Daniel will deliver you.

The Day After the Day After

After the fall of the Soviet Empire, we all saw what should have been a wonderfully encouraging sight: military men dismantling nuclear warheads, both in the East and the West. After decades of an exhausting and unnerving arms race, we were finally backing down from the brink of a nuclear holocaust.

But now another problem confronts us. Scores of nuclear scientists and technicians have suddenly become unemployed. How long will they sit idly by with so many nations eager for their expertise? Is the world a safer place now? Or have we only exchanged fewer bombs on the planet for more bomb makers?

On Sunday, November 20, 1983, 100 million Americans gathered in front of their TV sets to watch ABC's multi-million dollar movie—*The Day After*—a television dramatization of how America might look following a nuclear exchange with the USSR.

The huge viewing audience—the largest in TV movie history—witnessed a realistic vision (within limits, of course) of the impact of nuclear war on the residents of a small town near Kansas City.

In one particularly dramatic scene in the film, a mother hanging out laundry witnesses Minuteman missiles streaking skyward as her two children stop playing on the lawn to stare up in open-mouthed awe.

Suddenly, the various characters in the movie realize the inevitable—if the Minuteman missiles are outbound, Soviet warheads must already be on their way inbound.

Moments later, *The Day After* depicts the sequence of two Soviet missiles striking the Kansas City area. A little boy in a field turns toward his father as a flash of light vaporizes them both. Nuclear flames engulf cars on jammed freeways in giant balls of fire.

During the final hour of the film, viewers see the results of radiation exposure. The area around the nuclear blasts becomes a tomb for the walking dead. Every person exposed to the contaminated air is dead or dying. These scenes of a nuclear holocaust as envisioned by scientists and physicists are unrelenting, bleak, stark, and more depressing than anything ever dramatized on the screen before.

But of course, that was ten years ago. Is the world a safer place ten years later? So much has happened! The changes in Eastern Europe. The dissolution of the Soviet Union. The dismantling of nuclear warheads. The growing role of the United States as a peace-keeping body. Many are wondering if nuclear war isn't a thing of the past.

It's true that the two major superpowers no longer directly threaten each other, missile to missile. We can all thank God for that. But tragically enough, other events have made *The Day After* more graphically real than ever.

Since the airing of that TV movie in 1983, our world has experienced the greatest peacetime nuclear disaster in its history. At Chernobyl, more than fifty thousand square miles were contaminated by radioactive material released when that nuclear power plant broke down. Tens of thousands died. Cities have been left as ghost towns. Land, air, and water have been contaminated. Officials in the Ukraine have buried over 1,000 tons of beef contaminated by radiation from Chernobyl.

Unfortunately, power plant accidents are just part of

the story. The April 13, 1992, issue of *U.S. News & World Report* printed a radiation map that has never before been released to the public. It pinpoints more than 130 nuclear explosions conducted mostly in European Russia for geophysical investigations. The article made this remarkable statement: "Communism has left the 290 million people of the former Soviet Union to breathe poisoned air, drink poisoned water, and all too often bury their frail, poisoned children without knowing what killed them."

Tragically, *The Day After* has already come for too many innocent people. And people everywhere are wondering if the reactor down the road is really safe. When it comes to nuclear power plants, human error can be incredibly disastrous.

Jesus Christ was right on target when He described the attitude of thinking people in our day with these words: "Men's hearts failing them from fear and the expectation of those things which are coming on the earth" (Luke 21:26, NKJV).

Perhaps one of the most ominous signs on the horizon is the instability of the Russian republic and its neighbors. A serious problem has arisen which is seldom mentioned. There are 14,000 nuclear scientists in the former Soviet Union who were part of its massive military complex. These days, those still working earn an average salary of ten to fifteen dollars per month. They just can't survive. The former regime guarded these scientists carefully in order to protect their nuclear secrets. But now they seem to have no important role to play in the new country.

What if smaller, but fabulously wealthy, oil-rich nations hire these scientists at huge salaries to develop nuclear programs for them? Observers have begun to realize that this is a real possibility today. What if these nuclear scientists began leaving the former Soviet Union in droves?

Another concern is that underpaid military personnel

could succumb to large bribes to turn the other way while some of Russia's 30,000 tactical nuclear weapons are removed from their bases and smuggled out of the country. Reports of several such disappearances have already surfaced.

Over twenty nations already have nuclear weapons programs. Many political analysts believe North Korea to be on the verge of constructing nuclear weapons. China has a well-developed nuclear program. Saddam Hussein was much closer to achieving nuclear capability than most Western political analysts had thought possible.

In the midst of all this we're hearing a great deal of talk about peace. Recently, Boris Yeltzin addressed fifteen nations in the United Nations Security Council and spoke confidently about continued disarmament for a safer humanity. In the United States we've been discussing what to do with the "peace dividend" for some time now.

But the sad fact is that, even as the old arch-adversaries dismantle some of their warheads, the nuclear club continues to grow and instability increases. Most ominously, as historians know, there have never been weapons made that haven't been used.

So we're living in very peculiar times. The cold war is over. There is a lot of talk about a new world of peace and security. And yet in many ways the nuclear threat has increased rather than decreased. *The Day After* may be closer than ever.

Now please listen to this. Bible prophecy predicts that just before the coming of Jesus the world will apparently become safer but in actuality become more dangerous. The apostle Paul declares: "For when they say, 'Peace and safety!' then sudden destruction comes upon them" (1 Thessalonians 5:3, NKJV).

Isn't it interesting that Jesus made this part of His prophetic scenario that heralds His second coming. Let's look at a few more details in the prophetic picture.

Revelation 11:18 presents one of the clearest passages in Scripture revealing where we are in the stream of prophetic events. There is an urgency about this passage. It could not have been true twenty-five years ago. It applies to this very moment in time. It is a passage of Scripture penned by the aged apostle John in the Bible's last book—Revelation—for a generation speeding toward the year 2000. "The nations were angry; and your wrath has come. The time has come for judging the dead, and for rewarding your servants . . . both small and great—and for destroying those who destroy the earth" (Revelation 11:18).

The words seem to jump out at you! "And destroy those who destroy the earth." Never before in the history of the human race has mankind had the capacity to destroy itself and the whole planet.

You may not be aware of how close we have come to nuclear war in recent decades. Anytime the heads of the Russian republic or the United States travel, they are accompanied by an aide carrying a briefcase of electronic controls. The Americans call it the nuclear football; it's essentially the ignition key that turns on all-out nuclear war.

The former Soviet Union has three operational sets of such devices. The Russian president has one that can be used only in conjunction with another set controlled by the defense minister. A third "briefcase" is usually guarded by the defense ministry and can replace either of the other two.

But something happened after the aborted 1991 coup in Moscow. Western intelligence lost sight of that third "briefcase." No one could figure out where it had gone. Did one of the Communist coup plotters have it? Officials were forced to think about the grave possibilities of some maniac launching a nuclear war. Fortunately, after some hours of anguish, this third set of controls turned up in the Russian defense ministry.

Never before in the history of the human race has so much power been placed in the hands of so few people. And unfortunately, those few are spreading around the globe. The prospect of terrorists, dictators, or lunatics deciding the fate of the world by gaining control of a nuclear arsenal grows each day.

Revelation 11:18 speaks to us in these times loud and clear: "He will destroy those which destroy the earth." These words reassure us that God will come and deliver His people before the human race destroys itself.

Now let's turn to one last part of the prophetic picture that's rapidly become reality today. In Matthew 24, Jesus speaks of rising unrest between the nations; He speaks of war, rumors of war, nation rising against nation, increased national disasters such as famines, earthquakes, and pestilences, rising crime and violence. And amid all these tragic signs Jesus then lists the final sign before His return. "And this gospel of the kingdom will be preached in all the world as a witness to all the nations, and then the end will come" (verse 14, NKJV).

The Bible indicates that just before the coming of Jesus, barriers inhibiting the proclamation of the gospel will be broken down and the good news will reach the whole planet.

Consider this for a moment. Can you think of any time in history when almost half of the world was suddenly thrown open to the uninhibited preaching of the gospel? That has just happened. Nothing like it has occurred in the history of missions. Overnight, it seemed, the vast, closed empire of Communism collapsed and doors to those countries swung open. Suddenly ministers of the gospel were everywhere—Poland, Siberia, Bulgaria, even Albania— proclaiming the Word in churches and stadiums and government halls.

Jesus' prophecy echoes loud and clear, penetrating past the former iron curtain today. Despotic regimes can no longer hold His Word back. Like apple blossoms bursting open on a warm spring afternoon, the seeds of truth burst open everywhere.

The changes that have swept through Eastern Europe and the Soviet Union are not merely the result of political maneuvering. They are not simply the outworking of democratic political forces. There is a divine hand at work. God has opened doors miraculously.

For the past seven years I have conducted large evangelistic meetings in capital cities throughout Eastern Europe. Thousands have attended our meetings in places like Budapest, Hungary; Gdansk, Poland; Belgrade, Yugoslavia; and Moscow.

I was absolutely amazed when I preached in the former Soviet Union. I have never before seen such a hunger for the Word of God. Masses of people from all walks of life attended our evangelistic meetings: KGB officers, university professors, bank executives, government officials, physicians, and journalists.

In our recent series in the Kremlin Congress Hall, over 20,000 individuals attended. We offered a Russian Bible to anyone who attended at least four presentations. In two days we ran out of our supply of 12,000 Bibles. We purchased 5,000 more and again ran out. The audience completed 350,000 Bible lessons in just five weeks. Our staff was overwhelmed with this response to Bible teaching.

A spiritual revolution is sweeping through what used to be a vast Communist empire. And I believe there isn't a force on earth that can hold it back. This is the moving of the Spirit of God. This is the gospel dramatically going to all the world.

We are living in incredible times. Two kinds of knowledge are increasing and spreading over the globe today.

One is the knowledge of mass destruction; more and more countries coming up with the bomb. The other is the knowledge of human redemption; more and more countries are opening up to the gospel.

One kind of knowledge, the spread of nuclear technology, can produce the horrors of *The Day After*. The other kind, the spread of the Word of God, will bring on the glories of the Day After the Day After.

I believe that the knowledge of Jesus Christ is what counts in the end; it will win out in the end. It is a hope much more certain even than the prospect of that mushroom cloud hanging over us. The hearts of those who know Jesus are not failing for fear. Jesus Himself gave His disciples this assurance: "Let not your heart be troubled; you believe in God, believe also in Me. In My Father's house are many mansions; if it were not so, I would have told you. I go to prepare a place for you. And if I go and prepare a place for you, I will come again and receive you to Myself; that where I am, there you may be also" (John 14:1-3, NKJV).

The return of Jesus runs as a golden thread through the Scriptures. Each of the Bible writers looked forward with eager anticipation to that glorious day. Someone has counted 1,500 references to the second coming of Jesus in the Bible. For every prophecy about the first coming of Jesus in the Old Testament, there are eight prophecies about His second coming.

The psalmist declares, "Our God shall come" (Psalm 50:3, NKJV). The apostle Paul adds, "The Lord Himself will descend from heaven" (1 Thessalonians 4:16, NKJV). The angels present at Christ's ascension echo: "This same Jesus, who has been taken from you into heaven, will come back in the same way" (Acts 1:11). The apostle John, exiled on an island in the Aegean, joyfully exclaims, "He is coming with the clouds, and every eye will see Him" (Revelation 1:7, NKJV).

Throughout the world there is an expectancy of Jesus' coming. There is a sense that we are living on the verge of the eternal world. The whole world will soon be illuminated with the glory of God.

The stage is set. Our Lord is coming! Soon Jesus will descend down the corridors of the sky. Imagine the scene.

The darkened heavens are illuminated in a blaze of glory. Lightning flashes from the east to the west. Surrounded by tens of thousands of brightly shining angels, our Lord descends. The earth trembles. A major earthquake sends the Richter scale into orbit. Cities are leveled. Devastation is everywhere! Graves are opened! The righteous dead are resurrected. Along with the righteous living, they ascend to meet Jesus in the sky. What a day! Loved ones separated by death meet again. Husbands and wives join hands in joyous ecstasy. Angels place babies in their mothers' arms again.

Transformed in an instant, health replaces feeble, sickened bodies. Pain is a thing of the past. Heartaches are gone. New life pulses through our veins. Ascending into heaven with Christ, we sing songs of gladness, hardly able to believe what is happening around us. We feel overwhelmed with a special kind of joy—the kind that lasts forever.

There is another group who see Christ come. As they look up into the sky and squint at this dazzling, glorious Being, they get a sense of His holiness and purity—for the first time. And they tremble. All they can think to do is run and hide. These are the ones who have rejected the good news and turned their backs on God's truth. In the glorious brightness of Christ's righteous presence, they are consumed. What a tragedy! They could have entered eternal life with God, but instead they enter a death that lasts forever.

Jesus appeals to you today, my friend. He desires to

save you; He wants you with Him on the Day After the Day After. He wants you in heaven with Him forever. He longs for you to be there.

Are there habits in your life you're not proud of? Is there some sin you've been clinging to? Christ invites you to come to Him this very moment. He will pardon you. His mercy is yours. His grace will work powerfully to transform your life.

Will you open your heart to Him right now? He is the One coming again to take His people home. Only He can give you confidence in the midst of chaos.